Bristol Boy

Tim Fuller

Hoot Books Publishing
Owner, Victoria Fletcher
851 French Moore Blvd.
Suite 136 Box 14
Abingdon, VA 24210

CONTENTS

DEDICATION

This book is dedicated to my grandchildren.
My hope is that these stories will bring a smile
to your faces.

INTRODUCTION

Our lives are a story. Each person's story is unique, yet they are the same in one respect: each begins and ends with a breath. In between are millions of events: happy occasions (with laughter) and solemn ones (with tears), wise decisions we are proud of and foolish ones we often regret. Because we are made in the image of God, we are social creatures. We thrive on interaction with others. Relational behavior is in our DNA. We have an innate need to be a part of a group. The size of the group may be large or small, a national organization, or a neighborhood book club, but we must have contact with others. Isolation from others usually leads to tragic outcomes: many examples come to mind including numerous mass shootings at schools, Ted Kaczynski (the Unabomber), and Howard Hughes' last days. Even in our penal system we find "solitary confinement" which is simply punishment upon punishment. It's undeniable that human interaction is good for us. One of the primary things that take place when people interact is storytelling. Whether around a campfire or a kitchen table, stories (our lives) are shared. So, this is my story, at least a portion of it. I'm closing in on 72, and most of my life has been lived. If I were to compare my life to a football game, I'm halfway through the fourth quarter. I've had a great life, in part due to being an American and having the opportunity to spend a substantial amount of my life in southwest Virginia. So, pull up a chair, silence your cell phone, pour yourself a cup of your favorite beverage, and let's begin our journey back in time to the 1960s in Bristol, Virginia.

CHAPTER ONE

Comic Books and Cornbread

I was born on January 26, 1953, in Fort Shelby Hospital in Bristol, Virginia. My parents were Guy A. Fuller, Jr. and Joyce Nave. The hospital is now an assisted living facility named Fort Shelby Manor. It began in 1940 and closed as a hospital in 1955. My dad told me that he dropped off mom at the hospital in his 1948 Ford and picked her back up two days later holding a baby in her arms. I can't verify the truthfulness of that story, so I guess you and I will both have to go along with it. It probably happened like that because home births at that time were becoming a relic of the past. In the U.S., there was a huge shift towards hospital births beginning around 1900. Prior to then, almost 100% of births occurred at home. By 1938, the rate was near 50% and by 1955 was less than 1%.

I was the first of two sons born to Guy and Joyce. My brother Dave was born in Jacksonville, Florida on December 8, 1954. The reason he wasn't born in Bristol was because dad was working for various companies and my folks moved a lot around that time. They eventually ended up in Metairie, Louisiana around 1956, when dad landed a good job selling medical supplies in the New Orleans area. Some of my earliest childhood memories began there. I went through kindergarten, first, and half of second grade in Metairie. I can remember going to Mardi Gras parades with Al Hirt playing his trumpet on a float. I also recall riding in the backseat of our family car as dad drove down Bourbon Street. As we passed numerous night clubs, dad would say "you boys just keep looking straight ahead." I fell in love with red beans and rice which were regular menu items at school. We lived a few blocks from the elementary school I attended, so I would walk to and from school each day. One day, the main gate wasn't open for some reason and I didn't know how I was going to get in when suddenly some older boys said they would lift me up and over the chain link fence which surrounded the premises. Bowing to peer pressure, I let them hoist me up but as I sorta fell over the top, I ripped the leg of my trousers. Mom wasn't very happy when I got home that day and told her what had happened. Another event that was memorable was driving across Lake Pontchartrain. The Lake Pontchartrain Causeway is not only the longest bridge in Louisiana, but also the longest in the U.S.A. The southern end is in the suburbs of New Orleans, while the northern end is on the north shore of the lake. It's 24 miles long and goes across the middle of the lake. It's so long that when you get halfway across you can't see land in either direction. All that is visible is water on both sides of the bridge. For a young boy this was quite thrilling! The famous trolley cars of New Orleans were operating as mass transit back in those days and we rode them often. I had my first hospital experience while living in Metairie; I had my tonsils removed. I remember that all I was allowed to eat for a few days was Jello and ice cream. I was living every kid's dream! Besides the food, I was given a lot of gifts by folks who would visit. One of the best gifts was a Zorro action figure complete with cape and horse. Well, after five years in Metairie, dad grew tired of driving through rain flooded streets and going around the house every evening killing mosquitoes with a rolled-up newspaper.

Saying goodbye to New Orleans, we moved back to Bristol around 1960.

My education continued at Robert E. Lee Elementary School on Oak Street. Sadly, it burned down in 2023 after being vacant for almost a decade. It was there that many great memories happened, including my first childhood crush. Her name was Carolyn and besides being cute, she was fast! On the playground during recess, or while playing kickball, I could never catch her, although I gave it my best effort. Occasionally, when we had square dancing in the gymnasium, I would get her as a partner and boy was that a treat! Holding her hand was bliss.

It was in third grade that one of my teachers would read to the class *The Adventures of Tom Sawyer*. How mesmerizing it was to imagine what you were hearing as she read chapter after chapter. From the opening chapter with Tom painting the fence, to getting lost in the cave with Becky, it was magical to me. I began to develop a love for reading which has continued to this day.

My second experience with hospitals happened when I was in the fourth grade. I got pneumonia and was in the hospital for 2 or 3 days. I can remember how intensely it hurt if I took a deep breath. It felt like an ice pick was being jabbed into my ribs, or so I imagined. A laugh or cough or especially a sneeze was terrible! Only shallow breathing was comfortable. I recall, too, how the hospital staff would wake me up in the middle of the night to give me a shot to help me sleep! I don't think things have changed much over the years.

While attending Robert E. Lee, my brother and I were staying with my dad's parents. They lived at 617 Pearl Street, just off Euclid Avenue. We walked to and from school each day. Our family was having a home built near exit 5 on Lee Highway in a newer subdivision called Briarwood. It took 6 or so months to build, and so, we were staying with my grandparents until it was finished. Life on Pearl Street was fun. Our grandmother, Polly, would always have plenty of PET ice cream on hand along with Wrigley chewing gum. Every day after school we would watch American Bandstand while eating popcorn. Polly didn't really approve of the show because she thought that it wasn't appropriate for young ladies to show off their knees in public, because knees were "the ugliest part of a girl's body." On Saturdays, we would watch Shock Theatre hosted by Boris Karloff. It was scary fun! We also enjoyed cartoons, the Lone Ranger, Laurel and Hardy, along with The Three Stooges.

Our grandfather, Guy Fuller, Sr., was into making home movies. He was always making films when he had free time away from running the Fuller Bus Line, which ran out of Bristol from the late 1930s until the early 1970s. Buses ran on a scheduled route from Bristol to Saltville and back each day. Regular stops included Abingdon, Glade Spring, Meadowview, and Emory. I think the fare was 50 cents each way. The maintenance shops were located on Piedmont Avenue where the Virginia Department of Health is today. The shops backed up to Beaver Creek. The buildings once stood where the Health Department parking lot is today. I can remember dad taking me there as a young boy. It was cramped, dimly lit, and smelled like oil and diesel fuel. Two or three buses were usually inside being repaired or having regular maintenance performed on them. A mechanic would occasionally crawl out from under a bus, his bib overalls covered with dirt and grease. The sights and smells were vivid and pungent. As I said, Guy Sr. loved making and showing films and he had a designated room down in the basement of their home used for showing movies. This mini theater was complete with a couch and a large screen. There was even a small projection room where his equipment was housed. It included the actual projector and shelves to store reels of film. All films back then were on metal reels which slowly turned as the film ran through the projector. As the movie was being shown, the top reel would slowly get smaller while the bottom one would grow larger. It was fascinating stuff for a young boy to experience.

The residence on Pearl Street was a gathering place for family, especially on Sunday evenings. Lots of relatives would congregate for a hearty meal which usually consisted of soup beans, cornbread, onions, and my dad's favorite— "chow-chow." There was iced tea, coffee, and milk to wash everything down.

Plenty of PET ice cream was always on hand for a cool dessert. Hershey candy bars were a hit as well. On the nights the whole gang would be able to show up, the place was bustling with five couples and at least a dozen kids milling around. I look back fondly on those times.

Growing up in Bristol in the early 60s was tremendous fun. There were school field trips to the Barter Theater in nearby Abingdon, as well as Bristol Caverns. On Saturdays, we would go to one or both of the movie theaters in downtown Bristol. Both theaters were on State Street. The main street in Bristol is appropriately named State Street because the dividing line between Virginia and Tennessee runs down the center of the street. The street runs east and west with the north side in Virginia and the south side in Tennessee. Bristol is unique for that reason; it has two mayors, two police departments, two separate transit services, etc. Growing up in Bristol, this dual feature came in handy for those living on the Virginia side. The legal age to purchase adult beverages in Virginia was 21, but in Tennessee it was 18. We rebellious youth would simply drive over to the Tennessee side of town to get some beer and try to avoid getting caught by the local authorities in Virginia while consuming it!

There were two movie theaters on State Street back then: the Cameo and the Paramount. They showed the latest films put out by Hollywood. On Saturdays, both venues had special movies for kids which we went to often. You could get in for only 10 Coca Cola bottle caps. There was a full-length feature such as *The Time Machine*, *Journey to the Center of the Earth*, *Forbidden Planet*, etc. as well as a serial film, usually a Western, which always left the hero in a precarious situation which would be resolved the following week. The popcorn, sodas, and the movies themselves were a weekly treat.

Moore Street downtown was significant in my childhood for a couple of reasons: a barbershop and a newsstand. The barbershop was located in the building that currently houses the Birthplace of Country Music Museum. I can recall sitting in the big chair with its leather armrests and metal footrests, while getting my "ears lowered." It was often common for me to nod off while the barber practiced his craft. It was just so relaxing to have to sit there quietly. What I wouldn't give for that experience again, especially in today's world of noisy cell phones and constant activity! The warm towel applied to the back of my neck was a wonderful final touch to the whole experience.

Diagonally across the street from the barbershop was a newsstand called Tate's News. Boy, did I ever frequent that place! Like so many boys my age, I was into comic books: Spiderman, The Fantastic Four, and a lot of others were my Marvel favorites. War comics included Sergeant Rock, and GI Combat. When it came to Westerns, my favorite was The Two Gun Kid. Comics back then were 12 cents when I started buying them, and like so many things from the past, I wish I would've hung onto them. I see them on sale now for $6.00 each! Mom or Dad would drive me down to the newsstand where I would quickly exit the car and run into the store and begin scanning the racks for the latest issue of my favorites. There was an elderly gentleman who ran the place, and he would watch me intently as I scanned the racks for comics. If I strayed too far from the comic book section, he would softly admonish me to return to that section. Looking back, I can appreciate his concern for my well-being. Needless to say, not everything on the shelves was suitable for a young boy to be looking at! A few blocks away from Tate's News was a wholesale store that, in addition to everything else for sale, had bundles of older comics which were much cheaper. I think a bundle of 24 was only $2.00! The top half of the front cover was torn off each comic and the bundle was tightly wrapped with string. It was exciting to go home with your treasure, cut the string, and see what kind of comics were in the bundle.

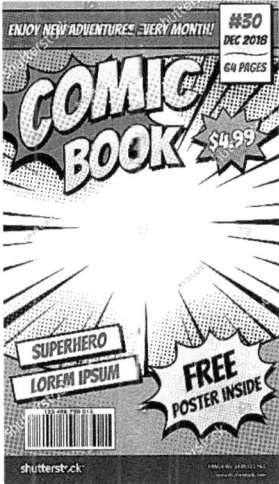

CHAPTER TWO

June Bugs and Pitchforks

After our house was finished, we moved in and our lives in Briarwood began. The earliest memory I have there was an event I refer to as The Crash. It was a perfect day in Briarwood. Perfect, that is, if you were a young boy at play with your brother. The summer day was hot with a clear blue sky, with only an occasional passing cloud to give some relief from the sun's rays. There was also a slight warm breeze blowing so a fellow didn't get too hot while he played. On this particular day, my brother Dave and I were engaged in our favorite activity: playing with our toy cars, trucks, and soldiers. We would construct roads, bridges, and forts in the red clay near our grandparents' house. Briarwood was just outside of the city limits, near exit 5. From our grandparents' backyard I could see for ten or more miles eastward up interstate 81, as it snaked its way up the valley, flanked by the Blue Ridge mountains on either side. Since the area was mountainous, Briarwood was naturally hilly. There were two roads that intersected our neighborhood:

Clover Lane and Haverhill Road. Our house was on Clover Lane and our grandparents' house was on Haverhill. Clover Lane ran due west from Lee Highway which was the major road until the early 60s, when the interstate came along. At the intersection of Clover Lane and Haverhill, if you turned right, you would then be going slightly downhill on a circular road aptly named "the circle" by all the neighbors. If you turned left instead of right, you went up a very steep hill which, at the top, curved to the right and then ran west similar to Clover Lane. This was Haverhill Road, and our grandparents lived right on the curve, first house on the right. That steep hill was where Dave and I spent most of our time. On one side of the street was an empty field full of tall grass, weeds, and a few bushes that at certain times of the year had wild blackberries growing on them. We didn't spend much time there except to pick some of the berries once in a while. For daring explorers like us, it was boring! The other side of the street, however, was awesome! A long dirt bank ran almost 30 yards until it ended at the four-way intersection formed by Clover Lane and Haverhill. Our dirt bank was not only long, but it was also at least

15 feet wide in spots. Plenty of room to build lots of roads, throw dirt clods at invading armies, or just slide down on the seat of your pants. On this day, however, we found a new use for our dirt bank. Somehow, we found ourselves in possession of an object which, by the end of the day, would grant us immense pleasure and equally immense discomfort. It was a little metal wagon, and yes, it was red. I can't recall where it came from or what happened to it later on; all I know is that it played a major part in the events that took place on this perfect day.

I guess we had been hard at play for a few hours when one of us came up with a brilliant idea: why didn't we get in the wagon and ride it down the street a ways? We would just go a short way down the hill and then steer the wagon up the dirt bank where the loose dirt would stop us quickly. Well, we tried it, and it worked like a charm! One of us would sit in front facing forward, gripping the wagon's long handle and using it to steer, while the other brave soul would sit facing towards the rear. The person in back would drag his feet to slow us down as we picked up speed. Each run down the hill became more and more of an adventure because we would go farther and faster each time. Gravity was our power source, excitement our goal, and an occasional stray dog our only spectator. Because the road was in use, we had to be careful and make sure the coast was clear before setting off on our downhill excursions. Since this was the early 60s on a rural road, traffic was intermittent, a car every five or ten minutes. This was ample time to make our short dashes which only lasted 15 seconds or less. The lure of a longer ride with more speed and distance began to beckon to us in a voice that only young, reckless boys can hear. I honestly don't know which one of us yielded to that voice first, but whoever it was needed only to mention the challenge to the other and it was instantly accepted with equal amounts of excitement and trepidation. This would be "the Ride," an event to tell sons and daughters about in the years to come!

The goal was simple; make it down the hill, through the intersection, and down the next hill which formed part of "the circle." So far, we had made 4 or 5 runs down the hill, each one ending with a run-off up the clay bank. This time, however, would be different. No wimping out and turning left. This one was straight ahead and just go for it! Because our speeds had increased on each of the previous runs, we decided to refrain from going all the way to the top of the hill to begin our record-breaking run (we were dumb, not stupid!). We pulled the wagon about ¾ of the way up the hill, turned it around, and gazed down the road. Convinced that the way was clear, we scrambled into our vehicle and positioned ourselves for takeoff. Dave was at the controls, gripping the wagon's long handle tightly between his knees to keep it steady. I was the brakeman, facing towards the rear, my feet firmly resisting gravity's tug as we prepared to go. Since it was warm, we were wearing only our shorts and tennis shoes.

As we began to roll, I was overcome with the thrill of it all. My heart was pounding in my chest, and the uncertainty of what would happen in the next few minutes was overwhelming! Our speed began to increase rapidly as I lifted my feet and tucked them into the apparent safety of the wagon. The places where we had aborted our other runs flashed by one after another, and for a brief instant I wanted to tell Dave to turn left and steer us up the bank once more, putting an end to this madness, but I remained silent as we raced on. Suddenly, a new sound and sensation became apparent. The small wheels of the wagon were wobbling as we neared the intersection at the bottom of the hill. The rapid, "womp, womp, womp" of the wheels was joined by the metallic groaning of the entire wagon as it struggled to handle these new laws of physics it had never experienced before. For a split second, I thought about jumping out, or at least sacrificing the soles of my feet to slow us down, but then tossed those ideas away and just gripped the warm sides of the wagon even harder. I could sense that Dave was having a difficult time keeping us under control because his entire body was shaking as the steering handle shook more violently the faster we went. Our backs were firmly pressed together and once or twice, the back of our heads bumped together as we sped along.

Then, all at once, we were racing through the intersection at breakneck speed (probably 8 miles an hour)! I wanted to give a shout of victory, but I heard Dave exclaim, "Oh no!" so I kept silent. I was truly puzzled. We had taken the dare, faced our foe, and pulled it off, so why was Dave not rejoicing? What did he see ahead of us? Then, all of a sudden, my questions were answered as I heard a loud "thud!" as our right front wheel hit a 3-inch-deep pothole that was directly in our path! The following sensations were strange to say the least. We were flying! There was no longer the constant bumping, swaying, and vibrating of the wheels on the pavement. I was now tumbling through the air silently, with only the sound of the air rushing past my ears. I saw Dave float by, turned on his side with a puzzled look on his face. Then I saw the red wagon upside down, outlined against the blue sky. From somewhere deep within me a voice asked, "How come you're not still in that?" Suddenly, my breath was knocked out of me, and I could feel the heat of the asphalt on various parts of my body, almost in the same instant. Then, all motion stopped, and I was lying on my side in the middle of the road. As I began to sit up, I saw Dave about 6 feet away as he too started taking inventory of his many wounds. I'm convinced there's nothing worse than road rash, except maybe burns. Both of us had the same kind of injuries; the only difference was their location and severity. Our ankles, elbows, palms, and knees were scraped free of skin. My worst injury was my right hip which I had obviously landed on. Where the skin used to be, there was now a patch of flesh that had a white color with untold numbers of little red dots beginning to grow larger by the second. I knew at once that this wound was going to be a lot of fun the next few weeks, especially at bath time. Dave's worst injury appeared to be his right shoulder. His "mark of valor" wasn't as deep as mine but covered a much larger area. We both got to our feet at about the same time, trying to appear brave, but tears started to roll down our cheeks. Neither of us cared if anybody saw them or not. Our great adventure on this perfect day had come to a less than perfect ending. We limped over to the wagon which was on the shoulder of the road. Turning it over, we slowly made our way back up the hill to grandma's house, where our wounds would be attended to.

This brush with death was the first of many in my rough and tumble childhood. The guardian angels of young boys sure have to work overtime! There were a bunch of kids in Briarwood when I was growing up. Since girls had "cooties," we guys sort of did our own thing and let the girls do theirs. Ours was playing sports and riding our bikes. Football and basketball were our favorite sports. The neighborhood was hilly, so riding your bike was a real workout. There was a small creek that ran through the neighborhood which offered all kinds of adventures: catching crawfish, snakes, or the occasional turtle. On one hot summer day, a few of us decided to dam up the creek. After shoveling a lot of dirt from the banks on both sides of the creek, the water level began to rise until the water reached our waists. The cool water felt wonderful. In constructing our "pool", we found a small snake when we pulled up a piece of sod. As I carried it home, it curled itself around my forearm. It turned out to be a great tool that I used often to scare girls! There was a small wooden shack in an empty lot that some girls used for a playhouse, and one day we caught a bunch of June bugs and placed them in a glass jar. Making sure the shack was empty, we opened the jar up and let them all out. It wasn't long before the girls showed up.

A few seconds after they went inside, we could hear them begin to scream and come flying out the door with a look of sheer terror on their faces! Besides playing sports, riding our bikes, and exploring the creek, we would toilet paper a neighbor's house once in a while, and one Halloween night we tossed water balloons over a row of bushes at a group of young trick-or-treaters.

One big event that happened in Bristol on a yearly basis was the Jerry Lewis Telethon. It was a nationwide event that raised money to fight muscular dystrophy. For a couple of years in a row, the local tv station, WCYB, brought in the cast of the hit show *Bonanza*. Each year there would be different actors from the show. The telethon would run around the clock as I recall. Once or twice, our parents took us down to the tv station to see the "stars" in person. It was cool to meet Hoss (Dan Blocker), Little Joe (Michael Landon), Adam (Pernell Roberts), and Ben Cartwright (Lorne Greene). It was big league stuff for us small town folks! The Telethon began in 1966 and was held on Labor Day weekend.

I started the 5th grade my first year in Briarwood. Since our subdivision was just outside the city limits, my brother and I went to Washington County schools. For the next 3 years, I attended Wallace Elementary. During my first year there, I was in an actual one room schoolhouse, complete with a coal burning stove in the center of the room. I can recall gazing out the windows at the cows grazing in the adjacent fields that backed up to the school property. It was hard to focus on learning as the arrival of spring was happening right outside the window.

Young boys sometimes have a lot of spare time on their hands, and I was no different. Soon after moving into our new home, I did a little exploring of my immediate surroundings. Since Briarwood was a new subdivision on the outskirts of town, we basically lived in the country. A short distance from our house was a farm where the Roark family lived. They were tenant farmers, which meant that they didn't actually own the place, they just lived there and managed it. It wasn't a large place, a small run-down house with a tin roof, a couple of old barns, and a concrete building where they dehorned cattle. I never watched a cow get dehorned, but from the bloodstains all over the walls of the building, I'm glad I didn't! I suppose that dehorning a cow is like trimming a dog's nails; if you clip them too close, they tend to bleed. From the looks of that building, some poor old cows had their horns clipped a might too close!

My first contact with these folks was rather one-sided. I couldn't resist throwing crabapples at their shiny tin roof! I was climbing a tree on the edge of our property when I first noticed their farmhouse in the distance. Well, I climbed down and picked up a handful of crab apples (crab apples are small, about the size of a quarter) and walked down the dirt road which led to their house. When I got about thirty yards from the farmhouse, I paused for a minute to see if I detected any signs of life. I didn't see anybody, so I let fly with a handful of apples. I hung around just long enough to see my missiles reach their target. The sound of the apples hitting the tin roof was extremely loud, and I was sure that if anyone was inside, they would come running out fast. I didn't stick around to watch but hightailed it back to the safety of my backyard apple tree. I stood behind it long enough to make sure the coast was clear. Minutes passed and nobody came charging out the front door. Everything was just as quiet as before my attack, so I assumed no one was home.

The Roark family consisted of the parents and their three children: Roscoe, Jerry, and Darlene. I can't recall the circumstances of meeting Jerry for the first time, but I remember seeing him ride a small, rusty bike back and forth on the street in front of our house on numerous occasions. Why this stands out in my mind so vividly is because the bike had no tires! Jerry would ride down the street with the metal rims making a terrible racket. You could hear him coming long before he came into view. Eventually, we got to know Jerry, who was close to our age, and soon we were hanging out on his property on a regular basis. I never set foot in his house, but we spent hours and hours playing in the barn. The ground level had stalls for animals, primarily calves and goats. The upper was full of hay bales neatly stacked row upon row. We had various games we would play in the barn. One we called "Alamo." We would pile up hay bales ten or fifteen rows high and try to climb up and "take the fort" from whoever was at the top. The enemy, of course, would resist our assaults and push or throw us back down. We would regroup and charge back up again. This would go for as long as we could muster up the energy and then all the tired combatants would call a truce and take a water break.

Another one of our barn adventures involved making tunnels in the hay and crawling around in them. The game went like this: one of the gang would take an old hat or some other clothing article and crawl into the tunnels and hide. The rest of us would try to find him and get "the trophy" away from him, which was easier said than done. One particular day, we were in the midst of this game when Jerry's dad came out of the house and into the barn. This was terrifying for many reasons: the "Old Man", as we called him, was nearly blind (Jerry had to help him shave) and he was mad because we had torn up so many hay bales during our games and he was carrying a pitchfork! He knew we played in the barn but had no idea that we had made tunnels and rooms in the hay. As he was climbing the ladder up to the loft, I could hear Jerry yell, "It's the Old Man, run!" I was crawling through one of the tunnels trying to listen and determine where everybody was and what my next move should be. Suddenly, it got very bright. Mr. Roark had been cursing and stabbing the pitchfork into the hay bales. Tossing one aside, I was lying there totally exposed! Needless to say, I was scared to death! Before I could say a word, he looked at me but quickly threw the bale of hay back on top of me. As he moved away, I was sure glad he had bad eyesight! I quickly crawled to one of the "escape" shafts and made a hasty exit out of the barn. I ran through one of the tobacco fields adjacent to the barn and rejoined the guys at the other barn. We were all excited and out of breath, but as the minutes went by, we began to laugh and tell our individual stories about our narrow escape from the "Old Man" and his pitchfork!

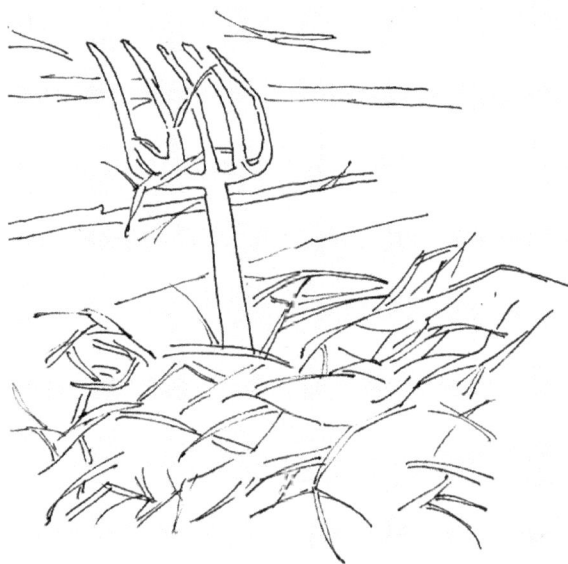

It seems like all of our games involved a certain amount of risk. Once, we made a noose with a rope we found and came up with a unique version of tag. If you were caught by the person who was it, you had to put the noose around your neck and stand on a hay bale until someone else got caught and took your place. It's a miracle one of us didn't get hung by accident! Sure, the barn was dusty and you got cuts and scratches from the bales of hay, but boy, did we have tons of fun!

I'm not sure how many acres made up the Roark property, but to a young boy it was vast. Besides the hay barn, there was another barn used for storing tobacco. There were a lot of woods and open pastures where some of the cows would graze. A horse had died and was buried in a spot in the field. Whoever buried it, failed to dig a deep enough hole, and as a result, a part of the decaying horse protruded slightly out of the soil. It stunk pretty bad, and if you stepped on it, it would make a strange sound and emit a nasty odor as well. As we made our way through the field, we would occasionally stop and step on the horse to hear the "hiss."

A short distance from the dead horse was a cave. The opening wasn't very large, so you had to sit down and slowly scoot down on your backside to enter the cave. Once you were ten to fifteen feet inside of the cave, you could stand up and walk around. There was a skeleton of some dead animal that someone must've thrown into the cave. It was a few feet from the cave's entrance. At the rear of the cave was a pretty good-sized room where we would all hang out. Hay bales were used to sit on, and candles were our only source of light. After spending some time making small talk, we would set fire to one of the bales of hay and see who could stay in the smoky cave the longest. Jerry always won, probably because he was the only one of the gang who smoked cigarettes.

CHAPTER THREE

Grapevines and Fried Potatoes

Around age 11, two significant things were happening to me physically: I began to have dental and vision issues. My primary teeth weren't falling out fast enough, so my dentist decided to extract them. For 6 weeks in a row, I had 2 teeth removed in order to make room for my permanent teeth. Obviously, that wasn't a fun 6 weeks. At about the same time, I began to have trouble seeing the blackboard at school. My teacher was concerned, so she sent a note home with me to give to my parents. Basically it said, "This child needs glasses." So, after a couple of trips downtown to see an ophthalmologist, I came home with a brand new pair of glasses! These glasses opened up a whole new world for me that I wasn't aware of. At home, standing in my upstairs bedroom, I looked out over our gravel driveway and instead of an expanse of gray, I now could see the individual rocks! Along with better vision, I now had the negative consequences of having glasses; taking care of them, which for an active young boy was a nuisance. I remember reading in a book at school a limerick that went like this "Leave adventures to the masses, take time to clean your glasses". That really ticked me off every time I read it. I wasn't about to slow down my pace of life or curtail my activities just because of those darn glasses! They did create some issues playing contact sports such as football or basketball, but damaged or broken glasses could always be bent back into shape or replaced.

We really liked to explore the woods that surrounded the Roark's farm. There were a lot of things one could do out there, including playing war games, swinging on grapevines, or having a cookout over an open fire. Our favorite meal was sliced potatoes cooked in butter with plenty of ketchup.

The most fun we had was swinging on grapevines while doing our best Tarzan impression. There was one spot in the woods that was our favorite for swinging on the vines. Down a sloping hillside was a large rock which we would use as a launch pad. You would grab the vine and run downhill and then launch yourself off the rock. Your intended landing spot was a tree limb about fifteen or so feet away from the rock. The limb was large enough to support the weight of one person at a time. Because it was 12 to 15 feet off the ground, you made sure you got a firm grip on it before you let go of the vine. Perched on the limb you were sorta stuck up there until someone would swing out to trade places. There were occasional instances where out of sheer meanness or bad timing, the "trapeze" exchange would not go as planned and things would get tense. Luckily, no one got injured during a mishap.

One day while enjoying the grapevine, we suddenly heard a very loud noise coming from somewhere in the woods. It could've been an old dead tree falling over, but whatever it was, it scared all of us nearly to death! We all ran down the hillside, across the dirt road, and over to the big tobacco barn. Scrambling up to its tin roof, we sat there waiting to see if some monster would emerge from the woods. After about ten minutes, we warily climbed down and hastily beat a path up to the safety of the farmhouse. To this day, I have no idea what caused that sound.

Winter activities in the fields were all about sledding. There was a tall hill that had no trees on it, so that was our favorite spot. We would spend hours there, trudging up to the top and then enjoying the 15 second ride back down to level ground. A fire was always burning to keep us warm.

Two girls close to our age lived in a house overlooking the sledding field. We spent quite a bit of time at their house shooting pool and riding their horse named Comanche. The horse didn't care much for being ridden. Once you climbed on his back, you were in for a short, fast ride until you fell off or were bucked off! There was no saddle, so you rode bareback with just a bridle and reins.

CHAPTER FOUR

Bicycle Races and A Silent Passenger

As time went on, we were very familiar with our neighborhood surroundings, so we began to expand our exploration. I had a classmate who lived a couple of miles north of our neighborhood, on the other side of the newly constructed interstate highway. There were two long drainage culverts that ran underneath the 4-lane highway. Both were concrete, square in shape, and had only an inch or so of water running through them on an average day. You could stand and walk through them as you crossed under the highway. We would travel through them to the other side and pass through a field and then a small grove of trees until we reached my friend's house. His dad had a wooden shed on the property which held tools, a lawnmower, etc. It also had a huge supply of fireworks stored inside. My friend showed us which boards to reach behind to gain access to them. Each of us would grab as much as our pockets would hold, and off we went, retracing our steps back to our neighborhood. The trip back resembled a war zone as we set off Roman candles, M80s, and tons of firecrackers!

In 1966, dad took a job flying for *The Kingsport Press*, a large publishing company in nearby Kingsport, TN. It was there that he met JT Putney. Putney was not only the chief pilot, but also a part-time competitor in Nascar sanctioned auto races. As soon as Dad began flying with JT, auto racing became a passion in our family, except for Mom. She rarely went to a race and complained about the fact that they were run on Sundays, and we would have to miss going to church. Dad, Dave, and I began to listen to the races on the radio on Sunday afternoons in the garage while Dad tinkered around with his cars. In 1967, we went to our first race at our local track, Bristol International Raceway. The track was built in 1963 and hosted two races a year. Our first race was the summer event won by Richard Petty. With this new racing fever in our veins, Dave and I transitioned it over to our bike riding. No longer did we just cruise around our neighborhood. Now every kid's driveway became a Nascar speedway! We would use stools, lawn chairs, or anything we could get our hands on to mark the boundaries of our "racetrack." We would entice the guys in our neighborhood to race with us by charging an entrance fee of 50 cents, which went into the pot and the winner got it all. The races were short affairs, 15-20 laps, with an occasional crash which resulted in broken spokes and scraped knees or elbows, sometimes both! The driveway races lasted for a time, but then we decided to go "big time." Adjacent to our house was an empty lot which was bowl shaped with one end steeply banked. That end made a perfect banked turn where we positioned the start/finish line. We cleared a lot of weeds, and soon we had a real dirt track to race on. We even made a pit lane where you could dismount from your bike and let your teammate take his turn, just like the famous Pony Express riders used to do. We made racing flags out of cut broom handles and different colored towels. Green for the start, yellow for caution in case of a wreck, white for the final lap, and of course, black/white checkered for the finish. The race distances were increased to as many as 50 laps since each bike had 2 riders. Soon, this grand production would have 6 to 8 bikes competing, while being cheered on by parents and other neighbors who would come out to watch the races, bringing lawn chairs with them to sit in. It turned into quite the event. One guy in the neighborhood had a small gasoline engine that he would mount on either a go-kart frame or a mini-bike frame. He entered one of the races and was literally wearing out the rest of the field until he lost control and dumped it on its side in the dirt. Leaking gas hit hot metal and the resulting fire brought all the action to a halt as 4 or 5 of us helped him put out the fire by throwing dirt on the mini bike! There was always a lot of drama during our races. We raced there until the day the lot sold and construction began on the future home that would soon be standing there.

Since our dad was flying for a living now, our life experiences often revolved around planes and airports. Dad had learned to fly as a young boy. He had a paper route in Bristol, and the proceeds went to pay for his flying lessons. On Sundays, weather permitting, he would hitchhike from his home to the local airport near Blountville, TN, a distance of about 11 miles. He would have to walk if rides were scarce. He was enamored with airplanes and was determined to become a pilot. As I mentioned earlier, his first job as a pilot was with *The Kingsport Press* as a co-pilot. That job ended after a few years and for a time he took whatever flying gigs he could find, including flying for the Forestry Service looking for wildfires. Funeral homes also used his skills on occasion. One such trip happened when I was at John Battle High School. It was a Saturday and dad asked me if I wanted to go with him to Tampa, Florida to pick up the body of a man and return it to Grundy, Virginia. Trips with dad were always an adventure in some form or fashion, so I agreed to tag along. We left the house early that morning and made the 30-minute drive to the local regional airport. The plane we would be using was a twin-engine model, with some modifications to the interior. There were two seats up front for the pilot and a passenger, but all the other seats had been removed. In their place was a long sheet of heavy plywood with a pair of seat belts attached in order to secure the body. We departed around 9:30 am, and after an uneventful 2 hour flight, arrived in Tampa.

We were met shortly after we landed by a hearse and two or three guys from the funeral home. They were pretty burly fellows, all wearing dark trousers and white shirts. The man who we were flying back to Virginia was an elderly gentleman who had died during surgery in a Tampa hospital. It was July, and extremely hot and humid. Just your typical summer day in Florida. As I watched, the men opened the back of the hearse and removed the body on a stretcher covered only with a white sheet! No coffin! I thought to myself, "Whoa, this is really weird!" The men carried the body over to the plane and placed it inside. One seat belt went across the corpse's chest, while the other across his lower legs. His head was uncovered and there was a block of wood shaped to cradle his neck. He was facing towards the rear of the plane, so his head was only about 18 inches behind our seats. I noticed a tag attached to one of his big toes, but it was too far from where I was sitting to be able to read whatever was written on it.

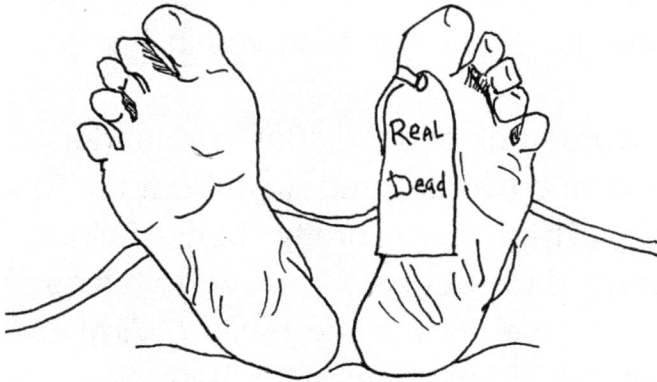

Once our passenger was secured in the plane, the sweaty guys closed the door and returned to the hearse, got in, and quickly drove away. Dad began going through his pre-flight checklist and attempted to start the engines. They refused to start! I think dad said something about "vapor lock" but whatever the cause was, he was able to fire the engines almost 2 hours later. We lifted off of the runway in the late afternoon and began the flight home.

Like most places, afternoon thunderstorms pop up rapidly in the summer months, especially in Florida. Dad was intently focused on dodging these towering storms as we made our way north. I had packed some sandwiches for our lunch, and after opening the paper bag they were in, I took one out to eat. Before I had taken my first bite, I happened to glance behind me at the body and noticed dark purple fluid coming out of his ears! It was the embalming fluid, and perhaps the altitude or cabin pressure was causing this strange occurrence to happen. Needless to say, I suddenly lost my appetite and put my sandwich back in the bag.

When we were approaching the Tri-Cities airport, it was almost sundown. Dad let me out and told me to wait until he returned in about an hour. The airport near Grundy wasn't as well lit as ours, and it was difficult to fly into after dark. For my safety, he wanted me to stay at the airport until he had delivered our passenger and returned. After he got back, we ordered a pizza to pick up on our way home. On the drive home, I asked him if the body had bothered him at all, and he said that most of the flight he was too busy flying and dodging thunderstorms to really pay any attention to our "silent passenger." Once he was alone in the plane on the way to Grundy, he said that he felt, "a little uneasy." I asked what his reaction would have been if he would've felt a hand touch him on the shoulder during his short, twilight flight to Grundy. He remarked, "Timmy, I would've opened my door and jumped out, parachute or not!" We both got a good laugh out of that!

CHAPTER FIVE

Smoke Bombs and Loose Teeth

Growing up in Bristol meant that on Sunday mornings, you went to church. We attended First Central Christian. It was located downtown until 1969, when it moved to its present location near the Stone Castle— a football stadium where Tennessee High School plays its home games. Our Sunday church-going routine went like this: Mom would drive the three of us to church (dad rarely went) and after arriving, Dave and I would put our ingenious plan into action. Dave and I weren't really into church, so in order to avoid an hour's worth of what we considered boredom, we did the following: first, we would observe where Mom and her parents were seated, and then as the service began, we would quietly leave our seats in the balcony and head to the Pastor's study. There we would be joined by the Pastor's son and a couple of other guys our age. Before we began discussing sports, cars, girls, etc., we would find the church service on the radio so we could hear the sermon being given downstairs in the sanctuary. We would listen long enough to get the basic gist of the message and then turn it off. Now, armed with mom's seating location and the basics of the Pastor's sermon, we felt confident to answer any questions that Mom might ask us on the drive home after service. Ross Dampier was the Pastor in those days, and I don't remember very many specifics from his sermons, except that he referenced Reformation Theology quite often, something I was clueless about. His son David was a good friend of mine, and we would spend hours together on Saturdays playing the board game Risk.

One particular Sunday, our group of miscreants were hanging out in one of the men's restrooms on the second floor, when one of the guys pulled out a smoke bomb from his pants pocket and proudly showed it off to everyone. It wasn't long until the dare was issued to "light it on fire and throw it out the window." After a brief hesitation, the fuse was lit, and it went sailing out of the bathroom window on its way to the ground. Since the church was newly constructed, there wasn't any grass yet, just straw-covered ground surrounding the whole property. If you're unfamiliar with how a smoke bomb works, I'll fill you in. Once the fuse is lit, it takes just a few seconds until the device is activated. An intense flame spews forth for about 5 seconds until the dark smoke is dispersed into the air. Fire and straw don't mix very well as anyone who has seen *The Wizard of Oz* can testify. We watched in horror as the straw quickly caught fire and began to spread rapidly! Acting quickly, we all ran out of the restroom, down the stairs to the ground floor, and out of the building. In a few seconds, we had stomped the fire into oblivion, but the black burn mark was a constant reminder of our folly for weeks afterward.

Young boys have a knack for getting into trouble, and an errand with our Uncle Paul was another such occasion. He took Dave and I with him one sunny afternoon to an automotive junkyard. It was huge, with acres of rusting cars and trucks lying around everywhere. While Paul was inside the office discussing the purpose of his visit with the owner, we wandered off down a dirt path amongst the mountains of wrecked vehicles. Boys are fond of throwing things, especially rocks. To this day I can't resist tossing rocks into a creek or lake. There's just some invisible force compelling you to pick up a rock and let it fly! Well, giving into the force, we began to search around for loose rocks and start tossing them at any unbroken windshield we could find. The air was soon filled with the sound of breaking glass! It wasn't long before Paul and the junkyard owner came racing down the path and quickly put an end to our fun. Paul was furious with us, and as we drove away, he threatened to, "Tell your Dad what you boys did today." I guess the old adage is true: "One man's junk is another man's treasure."

Summer heat usually drives one to some body of water to cool off, and that meant Crystal Pool for us. It was located north of exit 5 off of I-81, on the road that led to Wallace Elementary. The first few years that we went there, it had a large wooden structure adjacent to the pool. This was where you paid to get in, rent lockers, and purchase food and drinks. I recall a large plastic tub of water that you had to walk through to clean your feet before you were allowed to enter the pool area. Years later, that building was torn down, and a newer brick building was built to replace it. This new building wasn't as close to the pool as the earlier one was. It had a jukebox outside and a concrete slab for folks to dance or just congregate on. I went there often during my high school years, but it shut down sometime in the years that followed my graduation in 1971.

As previously mentioned, the guys in our neighborhood loved all kinds of sports, especially football. There was an empty lot that served as our all-purpose field. It was our baseball diamond and also our gridiron. Two significant events happened while we were competing on that vacant lot; one made me a hero while the other the "goat." One day our baseball game was halted when Mom drove up in our black 1959 VW Bug. It was one of dad's favorite cars. Dad also loved his 1948 Ford that he bought after WW2. He was on a waiting list for almost 3 years before he was allowed to get it. Anyway, Mom was going to the grocery store and wanted Dave or I to go with her to help her carry the bags. I was chosen and jumped into the car with her. She suddenly realized that she had left her purse at home, so she headed back to our house to retrieve it. She told me where to look for it inside the house, and when we pulled up the steep driveway and came to a stop, I hopped out. Suddenly, I became aware of a commotion coming from one of the upstairs bedroom windows. There, pounding on the window glass was my Aunt Dorothy, who was called Bayo (long story). She was shouting, "Your kitchen's on fire!" Mom and I both ran into the house and headed up the stairs to where the kitchen was. The stairwell was filled with smoke, as was the hallway. I was heading for the kitchen because we had a fire extinguisher mounted in the food pantry. Upon reaching the kitchen, I saw that most of the area over the sink was on fire and the burning curtains were lying on the floor. I opened the pantry, grabbed the fire extinguisher, and pulled the pin, just as Dad had instructed me to do. I took a couple of steps toward the wall of flame and squeezed the handle. As soon as the white powder hit the flames, they went out! It all took place in just a matter of seconds. By now the smoke was so bad, I could barely breathe, and my eyes were burning intensely. Running to the back door, I opened it to let the smoke out and to catch my breath. Mom and Bayo joined me in the backyard as the smoke continued to roll out of the back door which I had propped open. Mom had called the fire department and soon we could hear the sirens of the approaching fire trucks. About this time, a neighbor came out of a nearby house and asked, "Have a fire?" I was tempted to reply, "No thanks, we already had one" but I didn't. I was the hero of the day! One of the firemen told us that a few more minutes and the fire would have gotten into the attic. They set up large fans to help draw the smoke out. No water was needed, since I had put out the fire. I believe our family had to stay with relatives for a time until the kitchen was repaired. We never learned exactly how the fire started but both Mom and Dad were smokers and a smoldering cigarette butt was the likely culprit.

Now for the "goat" part… We all gathered at the lot for a football game one day and to our surprise, there was a carpenter at one end of "our" field. He was doing some work on the house adjacent to the field. He had parked his pickup truck smack dab in the middle of our imaginary end zone. This unwelcome object caused some consternation for a few minutes until somebody came up with a solution to the problem. Whichever team had the ball and was on offense would always start on the north end of the field, where the truck sat, and be constantly moving south, away from the truck. This worked wonderfully until my team recovered a fumble near our south end zone. Since we had almost the entire field to traverse, and it was first down, we decided it would be fine to run a few plays in the direction of the truck before we flipped field position and headed south once again. The only problem in our calculations was our play selection. The quarterback called for "the bomb" — a long pass down the field. I was a speedster in those days, so I was the wide receiver. The ball was snapped back to the quarterback, and off I went flying down the field in a blur. The quarterback dropped back a few yards from the line of scrimmage and heaved the football as far as he could. As it sailed through the air down the field, I managed to get behind the guy who was covering me and was in a great position to snatch the ball out of the air for a certain touchdown. Just as I reached out to grab the spiraling pigskin, I heard somebody yell, "Stop! Look out!" The next instant, I ran full speed into the side of the stationary truck! There was a loud noise, bright lights, and stars as I bounced 3 or 4 yards backwards, while my glasses and the football landed in the bed of the truck. Everybody rushed over to where I was lying to see if I was still alive and to render aid if needed. I laid on the ground for a while, regaining my senses, while somebody retrieved my glasses. I was wearing braces at the time (I wore them for a little over a year) and thanks to the braces, I didn't have any teeth knocked out. The wires were all twisted and had lacerated the inside of my upper lip pretty badly! Dave helped me up and into a car that was available. In a few minutes, I was home on the couch with an ice pack on my face. There were no broken bones or serious aftereffects, except that the trauma damaged one of my front teeth, which is dead to this day. Dave went back to the game after taking me home, and later that day he said the carpenter who owned the truck was angry because I had put a big dent in the side of it! I think he did call my parents threatening to sue us for damages, but I don't think anything ever came of it.

CHAPTER SIX

Midnight Visitors and Kidney Warmers

Since southwest Virginia is a mountainous region, outdoor activities abound, Camping is super popular. Once, our family decided to go camping in the Great Smoky Mountains, a few hours away. Arriving late in the afternoon, we were given one of the last remaining campsites by the park ranger. He informed us that this particular site had numerous black bear visits, and to be extra cautious and not leave any food out in the open at night. We had our supper around the campfire and probably turned in for the night about 10:30. We had two pup tents, one for Dave and I and the other for Mom and Dad. After zipping up my sleeping bag, I settled in for the night amidst the soft murmur of the other campers and the faint glow of the dying embers of our campfire. Sometime later, I awoke for some reason, and I sat up and got my wits about me. I saw a large dark shape walk by our tent, just inches away! Nudging Dave awake, we unzipped our tent flap and peered out. There, just 10 to 12 feet away from our tent was a bear standing on its hind legs while it tore into our cooler that was sitting on the picnic table! About that time, we heard Dad say, "You boys stay in your tent and be quiet!" Suddenly, other voices could be heard shouting, "Hey! It's a bear!" Just as suddenly as it had appeared, the bear was gone. We had lost a bunch of lunch meats, and a pound of bacon, but we had a wild story to tell everyone back home!

Since Nascar had become a big part of our lives, we traveled to different racetracks around the southeastern United States. On Labor Day, the Southern 500 was held at Darlington Raceway in Darlington, South Carolina. In October, we would often go to Rockingham Speedway in North Carolina. Dad had a younger brother named Jimmy who loved racing too, and he and his two sons would load up and go with us to these auto racing spectacles. We would camp, and unless there was a lot of rain, we'd have a great time. Nothing like camping in the woods and seeing the legends of Nascar battling it out on the high-banked asphalt ovals! We would camp at Myrtle Beach if we were going to Darlington, and close to Rockingham was a great little campground next to a small lake. Uncle Jimmy had a Sony reel-to-reel tape player which would run constantly with various country music legends like Charlie Pride, George Jones, and Glen Campbell just to name a few. Since it gets chilly in October for the Rockingham race, we brought along plenty of warm clothes and made sure the campfire was roaring at night. Dad had a best friend named Max Fullen who went with us on one of our

October racing trips. As we all turned in for the night, Max activated his "kidney warmers" and put one in each pocket of the coat he was wearing. These were small metal hand warmers that put out heat when certain chemicals were united. Shivering, he crawled into his sleeping bag murmuring, "Why did I let you guys talk me into coming?" Then, just like a scene out of Star Trek, he implored his wife Dot Allen to "Beam me up!" It was hilarious and the tent was filled with laughter as one by one we all began to doze off to sleep.

On another Rockingham trip, Dave and I were on the boat dock which jutted out into the lake. While we were waiting for supper to be ready, we noticed some ducks heading our way, so we began looking around for something to throw at them (that "boys throwing things" again). We found a few small stones in the dirt where the dock met the shore, and Dave wound up to hurl one at the ducks. All of a sudden, he tripped on a small block of wood that was nailed to the dock and into the lake he went! The water wasn't very deep so he somehow managed to keep one arm out of the water and dry. He waded to shore and since the sun was almost down, he was shivering due to the cold water and air temperature. Hustling back to the campsite, he got out of his wet clothes and hung them on a line to dry out. He got into some dry clothes and sat as close to the campfire as he safely could. The temperature dropped down to around freezing that night, and on awakening Sunday morning, his clothes were frozen solid!

In 1968, my favorite Nascar driver was Richard Petty. The Petty family had a long history of driving Plymouth automobiles stretching back to the early 50s. Each week, Petty, in his famous blue #43, would compete against a host of Ford drivers and usually end up in victory lane. In 1967, he actually won 10 races in a row before his win streak was broken. It was at the fall race at Charlotte, and we were there for our first trip to that track in hopes of seeing him win number 11. He was involved in a crash early in the race which ruined any chance he had at victory. Well, there was a female friend of mine who loved Nascar as much as I did, except that she pulled for the Ford drivers each week. Needless to say, every Monday was usually my time to rub it in with Petty's latest win. We were both students at John S. Battle high school and our first class together each day was time to brag or make excuses. I rarely had to eat any humble pie! That all changed in 1969 when Petty switched from Plymouth to Ford! I was devastated but she was elated. For one whole year I had to put up with her constant reminders of how Petty had "seen the light" and switched manufacturers. He only drove a Ford for that year and was back in Plymouths in 1970.

High school was a good time in my life. My strengths were in writing and history. I devoured almost a book a week, usually World War 2 or the Civil War. I also got into the James Bond series of books as well as Nero Wolfe detective novels. Math was not my thing, and I struggled with Algebra. I joined the wrestling team and also ran track. I wasn't great at either but I did win a few medals in some track meets. Getting my driver's license at age 16 was a game changer. Dating became a regular event and Mom and Dad were sure happy that they didn't have to drive me all over Washington County anymore to hang out with my girlfriends. Our family owned two VW Bugs back then, along with Dad's beloved 1948 Ford. One winter day Dad was getting ready to go on a flying trip and as was his habit, he checked out the weather for the day. Seeing that snow was in the forecast, he admonished us not to drive anywhere that afternoon. We agreed and he set out for the airport. Being a Saturday, we got bored and decided to go down to a record store on Commonwealth Avenue where our mom worked part-time. We left before noon and spent way too long in the store. Leaving the store, we noticed that it was snowing and the ground was getting covered. Remembering Dad's warning, we hurried to the car and headed home as fast as we could. As we drove on Euclid Avenue, I began to show off by swerving the car back and forth. Suddenly, I lost control on the snow and the car slid into the curb and hit a small tree next to the sidewalk! The impact wasn't much but enough to bend the front bumper slightly. Now we were dead meat! All afternoon we dreaded Dad's arrival, trying to come up with some excuse to exonerate ourselves but there wasn't any. We had disobeyed and now had to face the music. I'm not sure if we confessed or kept quiet about the incident but Dad found the damaged bumper soon and let us know he wasn't happy. You know, sometimes your parents know what they're talking about!

During my senior year at Battle, I was on the varsity football team. It wasn't a great team, but we played the Tennessee High Vikings pretty well at the Stone Castle that year. The Vikings were the national champs that year and crushed everybody they played— except us. We held them to only 20 points as I recall. David Halstead was our quarterback and Jeff Stanley the fullback. Levi Otey was the head coach. My brother Dave was also on the team that year and despite some bumps and bruises, we had a good time.

CHAPTER SEVEN

College Daze and Spiritual Haze

After graduating from John S. Battle, I decided on enrolling at Virginia Polytechnic Institute & State University (Virginia Tech). I had applied and been accepted to 3 different colleges, including Carson Newman, James Madison, and Tech. Since my Uncle Jimmy had gone to Tech, it wasn't really a hard decision, so, in the fall of 1971, I was off to Blacksburg, Virginia. I was a "Hokie!" What the heck is a Hokie you're probably thinking. Well, there's a bit of mystery surrounding how that word originated. In order to not cause your eyes to glaze over, let me explain it this way. The official mascot of the college in the early 1970s was a giant turkey or gobbler. The VA Tech Fighting Gobblers! Now, you're probably saying to yourself, "That's pretty hokey!" See, there's your answer! Anway, over the years the Gobbler has given way to the Hokie Bird as the official school mascot. When I was a student there, the scoreboard had an image of the Gobbler and every time Tech would score a touchdown or field goal, a strobe light in his eye would flash and a loud "gobble, gobble" would be heard over the loudspeaker! Football games were a hoot, or dare I say… gobble? After getting textbooks, signing up for classes, and moving into a dorm, life settled down to the weekly grind of being a student. Monday through Friday was mostly about academics, but the weekends were all about having fun. There were football games and concerts to go to, as well as intramural sports to participate in. I played flag football my first year on campus and had a fun time without any injuries, which is more than a lot of students could say. There were two or three ambulances stationed around the playing fields during events because there were always broken bones and other injuries occurring, even though it wasn't tackle football. College age guys play rough!

My roommate in my freshman year was Jimmy Flippen. He was a laid-back sort of fellow, very low profile. He was from nearby Roanoke, VA and had a 1965 Plymouth Barracuda. One cold February day, I was reading in a local newspaper about the upcoming Daytona 500 and wishing to be warm for a few days, I asked Jimmy if he'd like to drive down to see the race.

He mulled it over for a couple of minutes and agreed that it would probably be a fun thing to do, so he was in! We left school on a Friday afternoon, as soon as all our classes were over, and headed to his home in Roanoke to get some food and sleeping bags for the trip. After a long 12-hour drive, we pulled into the parking lot of the Daytona International Speedway complex. It was late afternoon on Saturday, and a 300-mile race was underway, so we had to wait until it was finished before we were allowed into the infield. We drove into the massive infield area and found a spot on the grass between turns 3 and 4. If you've ever been to Daytona in February, you're probably aware that it can get downright chilly. It was only in the high 40s around sundown and the lows were forecast to dip below freezing overnight. As the evening approached, people were starting fires in grills, barrels, and on the ground to ward off the cold. All we had were a couple of light jackets and our sleeping bags. After all, we thought we were going to be in warm, sunny Florida for the weekend! We even brought our swim trunks along in case we had the opportunity to go for a dip in the ocean. Boy, did we guess wrong! The temps got down to 29 degrees overnight, and we woke up shivering around 2 am. Jimmy decided to start the car and let it run for a while so that we could use the heater to get warm. This would have been a good idea if only he hadn't fallen asleep behind the wheel with his foot on the gas pedal! I woke up choking from the exhaust fumes, and waking Jimmy up, we both quickly opened the car doors and exited the vehicle into the frigid early morning air. Now we could breathe again but were instantly freezing in our shorts and light jackets. Getting back into the car, we agreed that one of us would always be awake, and that we would run the car for only a few minutes at a time until daybreak. Sunrise brought a gradual warming, and by the time the race got underway, the temps were in the upper 50s. Another thing we learned was that you can't see much of the race from the infield. We could only see the cars for about 5 seconds as they zoomed by at 190 mph on the high banked turns. We didn't have a portable radio with us so unless we sat in the car, we didn't know what was really happening in the race. At one point, there was a spectacular crash on a part of the track that we couldn't see, and eventually the race was won by AJ Foyt.

Leaving Florida, we vowed to never do the 500 that way again!

During my second year of college, I changed roommates and learned how to scuba dive. Wayne Vick was a really tall guy from Franklin, Virginia, which is on the east coast near Norfolk and Virginia Beach. He drove a late model Camaro which we took on some long trips to see some concerts, and visit Farmville, Virginia. There was a girl from Bristol I knew who was attending Longwood College located in Farmville. Well, Wayne and I were both interested in learning to scuba dive, so we joined the Virginia Tech Scuba Club. After buying our equipment and going through all the training, we were ready to take our newfound skills to the open water. We found out about America's first underwater park, John Pennekamp Coral Reef State Park. It is in Key Largo, Florida and encompasses 70 nautical miles, all underwater! Wayne's family owned a small boat and we, along with a fellow classmate named Steve, made the late summer trip to Florida to dive for 3 or 4 days. We had a fantastic time and vowed to top that adventure during Spring Break by flying to the

Bahamas for a few days of diving. Pooling our resources, we chartered a plane to fly us from Ft. Lauderdale to Andros Island and back. We drove to Florida and back after spending 3 fabulous days enjoying the seafood and diving at the Andros Beach Hotel and Villas. One evening during a relaxing meal at sunset, I remarked to the guys, "If I ever get married, this is where I'm coming for my honeymoon." Little did I know that three years later, I would be doing exactly that!

Besides having fun away from college, I had plenty of good times in the dorm as well. There was a short Jewish guy down the hall from us named Gary Rosenthal. He was high strung, always animated, and just an interesting fellow to interact with. One day, I snuck into his room and crawled under his bunk bed while he was out in the hall chatting with some other guy. Well, in a few minutes he returned and as he stood beside the bed, I reached out and grabbed his right ankle while trying to do my best barking dog sound effect! It scared the daylights out of him! His roommate later told me that he must've jumped two feet high before dashing out of the room, with a look of sheer terror on his face! Besides playing pranks on folks, other exciting things would happen out of the blue. One evening I was sitting by our window watching the sun go down, when a bottle rocket came whizzing by my head and smashed into the brick wall next to the wooden window frame! Startled, I began looking around the courtyard below to see who had attacked me. For the next few minutes, I felt like I was in Fort Sumter! I lived in Major Williams Hall which was shaped like the letter L. In the other wing of the building in a stairwell, I saw 3 or 4 guys firing the rockets at our side of the building. With no way to retaliate that day, I closed the window and vowed to enact my revenge in the future. Purchasing a slingshot and a supply of bb's, the next day I couldn't wait for round two of their attack. I didn't have to wait long, as a short time later the air was again filled with hissing rockets trailing smoke as my enemies resumed their attack. This time I was ready for them. I hurriedly grabbed my slingshot, that had never been fired, and in anger loaded it with 3 bb's. Leaning out of my third-floor window, I let fly a barrage of bb's at the 2nd floor stairwell where my foes were launching their assault. I must've hit at least one terrorist because I heard painful cries from the group! The battle raged for 10 to 15 minutes until some authority figure broke up the action in the stairwell, ending the conflict as suddenly as it had begun.

Even though I was an okay student, as far as my grades were concerned, I began to have deep concerns regarding my reason for being at college in the first place. I was almost halfway through my 4 years at Tech, and I didn't have a clue as to what I was going to do after graduating. My major was Sociology/ Psychology which I declared as an incoming freshman, in large part because it sounded cool. I had no idea what my job prospects would be after college. I was there to have a good time and stay out of Vietnam. I had started dating a girl back in Bristol named Pam and our relationship was getting rather serious. The thought of marriage and having to provide for us and any children in our future began to weigh heavily on me. One day, as my troubled thoughts seemed almost overwhelming, I said to God, "Lord, you made me and you know what's best for my future. If you'll show me the truth about life, I'll do whatever it is that you want me to do." I knew at that moment that I was now on a spiritual quest, not knowing where it would lead me. I began to read the Bible and not knowing where to start, I began with the New Testament book of Matthew. I believed deep down that the Bible was true but never having read it diligently on my own, I was a novice.

As my second year at Tech was winding down, I decided not to stay at college and didn't enroll for my Junior year. I returned home to Bristol and got a job working at Bristol Steel. Pam and I talked about our future plans together. She was a senior at John Battle and marriage in the near future for us was not an option. The only plan I came up with was to try to find work in Florida using my interest in scuba diving and photography. With the money I had available, I bought a bus ticket as far as Spartanburg, South Carolina and then hitchhiked the rest of the way to Miami, Florida.

CHAPTER EIGHT:

Rough Seas and Frog Legs

Having been to Andros Island recently, I was ready for a return trip. Purchasing a one-way ticket to Nassau, the capital of the Bahamas, I soon was winging my way eastward over the blue waters as I departed Miami International Airport. Once in Nassau, I made my way to the boat docks in the harbor. There were daily boats that left Nassau for the "out islands." These various ships were called "mail boats" since they carried mail along with just about anything that had to be sent to some other island. Items included food, generators, gasoline, live animals, and even people. If it was needed or wanted, there was a boat to get it there! One boat was leaving around 10 pm for Andros, so I inquired if I could book passage. The captain of the boat said that there was no need to buy a ticket, I could just help with loading it in exchange for a ride to Andros. I quickly accepted his offer, and for the next three or four hours, I helped load all kinds of stuff from the dock onto the ship. Our task was completed about sundown, and we all sat around the deck while dinner was served by a crewman. It was basically a bowl of rice with some beans and chicken mixed in. Having had very little to eat since that morning, I was hungry and finished my first bowl off in no time! Seconds were the same ingredients, just a smaller portion. The two or three crew members finished tying barrels down and doing other pre-departure chores, while I went below decks to my assigned bunk and lying down, I dozed off as the busy day took its toll.

A short time later, a deep rumbling sound jarred me awake, as the boat's engine came to life. Scrambling up on deck I saw a crewman pushing the boat gently away from the dock with a pole of some sort, and slowly we began to ease our way out into the harbor. As the boat glided across the moonlit waters, I was overwhelmed by it all. The sky was filled with stars and the gentle rhythm of the engine was reassuring. I felt a wave of exhilaration wash over me! I was nervous and at peace all at the same time.

After an hour or so of gazing into the darkness that surrounded us, I began to grow sleepy and decided to retire below decks. The combination of the murmur of the engine and the swaying of the boat through the sea soon had me fast asleep.

I was awakened by the tremendous rolling and shaking of the whole ship. A storm had snuck up on us in the middle of the night and now had us in its grip. I rolled off my bunk and bracing myself with both feet and arms, I managed to climb the four steps up to the pitching deck. The sight that greeted me was wild! Waves were crashing against the ship and the seawater was washing over the sides as the captain tried valiantly to steer into the waves. The wheelhouse was in the center of the ship closer to the bow. It was illuminated and I was watching the captain's back as he gripped the massive wheel. He was dressed in white trousers and shirt, which was in stark contrast to his coal black skin. He was barefoot as he turned the wheel left and right in his battle with the storm. He would bark out commands every so often to one of the crew. They were scrambling all over the stern in a desperate attempt to prevent loose items from falling overboard. They failed at one point as two large drums rolled from one side of the ship to the other and fell overboard into the churning sea. I watched them for about a minute, bobbing in the swells until the darkness claimed them. I sat down with my back pressed up against the wheelhouse in order to not risk falling. All I could think of was that I had come all the way from Virginia just to drown at sea! Nobody I knew had any idea of my predicament. My poor parents might never know for sure what my fate was. Beginning to feel queasy in the pit of my stomach, I decided it was time to retreat below decks to the relative safety of my bunk. Climbing in, I stared at the bunk above me and gripped the sides of the bed to keep from falling out. I must have fallen asleep rather quickly because the next thing I knew the boat was gently swaying back and forth like before the storm. I hopped out of bed and reached the upper deck. I could see that the rain and wind were gone, and the sun was attempting to break through the remaining clouds. In the distance, I could dimly make out the shore of an island that I assumed must be Andros. It was, and within 30 minutes we were docked, and the crew were beginning to unload. Saying goodbye to the captain with a smile and a wave of my hand, I headed inland.

I learned that I was four or five miles from the hotel where Wayne, Steve, and I had stayed two years earlier. I started walking along a one lane paved road which was flanked on either side by tall marsh grasses. Even though it was November, it was really hot and mosquitos were a real nuisance. I was carrying a pretty heavy backpack with clothes, mask, and fins, etc. and I was getting thirsty as the road seemed to go on forever. At one point I said, "Lord, I sure could use a car to come along right now!" Within a few minutes, a car came up behind me and stopped. Soon I was rejoicing as we sped away towards my destination!

Arriving at the small community which surrounded the hotel, I asked around about accommodations and eventually ended up talking to a couple from Germany. They had bought a one room stone cottage a few years back and had an acre of land. They had a small one-man tent a short distance from the cottage that they used to keep their overflow items in. They graciously said that I could stay in it for the duration of my time on the island. I stayed on Andros for about eight days. I would spend my days strolling along the white sand beach and spearfishing offshore. Any fish I caught were donated to my hosts to help with our dinner meals. I would usually buy some chicken and a soda for my lunch each day after the three of us would have breakfast. Some guys I met took me out into deep water for some serious fishing a couple of times during my stay. The German couple's names were Theo and Carol. A few conversations happened as they noticed my Bible reading. They told me that they were both atheists but were okay with my spiritual seeking. It was basically a "live and let live" agreement we had. Life was laid back and cheap, but I realized that I wasn't making any progress towards finding a job, so I decided it was time to leave "paradise" and get back to the real world on the Florida mainland. Saying my goodbyes to everyone I had met in my short stay, I caught a ride to the small local airport, purchased my one-way ticket, and in no time, I was headed back to Miami.

The flight from Andros to Miami was short due to the close proximity of the Bahamas to Florida. Upon my arrival at Miami International Airport, I took a quick look at my finances and decided to make a phone call to my folks back home. I had left $200 in reserve with my parents and thought now would be a good time for them to wire the funds to me. While on the phone with them, they told me about some relatives in the Miami area and gave me their phone number. I thought that giving these people a call was the way to go, so I hastily dialed their number (pre-cell phone days, we all had to use public pay phones). Time has erased their names, but I do remember that the wife answered the phone and after hearing about my situation she said she would send her husband over to pick me up. She insisted that I spend the night at their place, so I gratefully accepted her offer.

Within 20 to 30 minutes, a large 4x4 pickup truck pulled up next to the curb and as I stepped towards it, I noticed the driver was a huge guy wearing a CAT (short for Caterpillar, as in diesel, oh, just forget it) ball cap. The good Lord certainly has a sense of humor because the two of us were as different as night and day! I was a young, skinny, long-haired (yes, I really did have long hair back then) religious hitchhiker dressed in old army fatigues and my rescuer was a gigantic, Florida "Cracker" (redneck) who owned his own bulldozer and was by his own admission, an atheist. He sized me up very quickly and it was obvious he didn't approve of what he was looking at. For an instant I thought he was just going to drive off, but he just snarled "Git in" as he opened the door. I hesitatingly climbed in and off we went. There was dead silence practically the whole way to his house and I kept thinking to myself, *What in the world have I got myself into now?*

Well, he didn't kill me; in fact, I actually stayed with this couple for close to six weeks. The three of us got along quite well. The husband even took me out to the everglades one evening to go "froggin." He had an airboat which he used to catch frogs with. All he was after was the frog's legs so he could sell them to the local restaurants and make some extra money. If you've never seen an airboat, I'll briefly describe it: picture an aluminum boat with a tall seat in the middle of the boat with a huge propeller behind it. The driver sits up high on the seat with a long trident in one hand and the controls to the boat in the other. On his head is a powerful lantern which is used to spot the frogs as they sit on the vegetation floating on top of the water. When the operator spots a frog with his light, the frog freezes due to the brightness of the light. This, of course, makes the poor frog a sitting duck, or should I say frog? The hunter then only has to spear the frog as it sits there, pretty simple if I do say so myself. Well, we were out all night in the swamp circling around and around "gigging" frogs. He had a large mesh bag that was attached to his seat and after he had speared the frog, he would pull it off the end of the spear and toss it into the bag. I was sitting fairly close to the bag and after four or five hours, the bag was full of dead or dying frogs, which began to give off some really unpleasant odors! Come daylight, the hunt was called off and we returned to dry land where more horrors awaited the poor frogs. He would take each frog and place it on a huge tree stump and with a hatchet neatly sever its back legs from the rest of its body. After watching a couple of frogs meet this sad fate, I went looking for something else to do till the ghastly event was over. To this day I have not, nor ever will, eat frog legs!

In exchange for a place to sleep and three meals a day, I agreed to paint the exterior of their house. They both were very large people and no wonder; at each meal the wife would fix enough food to feed a small army! I ate so well I must have gained at least five pounds during my stay. The husband had recently suffered a heart attack and could only walk short distances before he was forced to sit down and rest due to shortness of breath. He was self-employed but hadn't worked for three months due to his health. He owned a bulldozer which he used to clear land on construction projects, but since his heart attack the dozer had just been sitting on the trailer and he was worried about not being able to make the payments on it. I longed to tell them to ask God to act on their behalf but like the German couple on Andros, these folks told me they didn't believe in any kind of God but if "it worked for me that was okay by them." I remember one night after dinner as I was helping to clean up, the wife told me that she liked Johnny Cash's music but now that he had become "religious" and recorded a Gospel album, she wasn't so fond of him anymore. She said she preferred "the Man in Black."

A short time after I began to paint their house, a very significant event happened. It was late in the day, and I was on a ladder painting some trim around one of the windows, when a middle-aged lady and a teenage girl came walking up the driveway towards the house. They began to knock on the front door and soon the wife came and let them in. After a short while, all three of them came back outside and walked over to where I was painting. The wife introduced them to me and turned to them and said, "He might be interested in going to your meetings because he's religious, too." The wife dismissed herself and went back into the house leaving the three of us to chat among ourselves. I found out that the pair were neighbors from down the street, a mother and daughter who just happened to be out for a short walk. They attended a small church in the area and wanted to invite me to a youth meeting held on Thursday nights. I said, "Sure, I'd love to go." We got all the particulars set about the time and place and they said it was great meeting me and that they'd see me in a few days. As they left, I couldn't help but think that maybe my spiritual search was about to be rewarded.

True to their word, the gals picked me up the night of the event and after a quick trip, we arrived at the church. The weekly meeting was called Youth Ranch, and the goal was to appeal to high school students as a means of introducing them to consider Christianity in a fun, non-threatening environment. The large room where the meeting took place was decorated in a western or cowboy theme including bales of hay for seating. Two guys with guitars led everybody in a few songs and after some announcements about upcoming activities, one of the guys opened up his Bible and began to talk. The years have erased most of what his talk was about, except what he shared in closing. This young man, a student at Florida Bible College in nearby Hollywood, told us the "good news" otherwise known as the Gospel, found in the pages of the New Testament. He explained that God was perfect, or holy, and people weren't. He quoted Romans 3:23 to prove that all of humanity was imperfect or "sinful." It says, "For all people have sinned and fall short of the glory of God." He went on to explain that the Greek word for sinned in the verse is "Hamartano" which means to "miss the mark." An example would be archery, where the goal is to hit the bullseye, yet the arrows are missing the center of the target. Because we are human, we can never be perfect (as God is). His holy nature requires that we become as He is in order to dwell in His presence. We need to be perfectly righteous. Our "goodness" as humans is relative. I may be a better person than you, or you may be nicer than your neighbor, but none of us measure up to God's standards; we all fall short. He then read a verse from II Corinthians. In chapter 5, verse 21 the Apostle Paul wrote, "He (God) made Him (Christ) who knew no sin, to be sin on our behalf, so that we might become the righteousness of God in Him (Christ)." Because of His great love for us, God became a man (Jesus) and voluntarily laid down His life on the cross so that we could be made righteous by accepting Christ as our personal savior. Christ died in our place. He took our punishment so that we wouldn't have to; we can go free.

Let me explain it this way: Suppose you are caught speeding and hauled into court. The fine is so high that there's no way you could come up with the money. You are looking at some serious jail time. Just as you are about to give up all hope of avoiding being locked up, the Judge does something really remarkable. He takes off his black robe and steps down from the bench. He then takes out his wallet and pays your fine! This is what God has done for us. We each have sinned in thought, word, or deed and we can't pay the fine— we're toast— but God through Jesus' death on the cross has paid our fine, and all we can do is accept what He has done for us by faith.

The Bible says that salvation is a gift. Romans 6:23 states, "... the free gift of God is eternal life in Christ Jesus our Lord." Gifts are by their very nature free. You don't pay for your own Christmas presents— somebody else already has! All you can do is receive the gift or refuse it. Those are your only options. One of my favorite verses is John 1:12. "But as many as received Him (Jesus) to them He (God) gave the right to become children of God, even to them that believe in His name."

That night it all became clear to me, all the spiritual puzzle pieces suddenly fit. As the speaker reached the end of his talk, he asked if anyone would like to know for sure where we go when we died. He then quoted I John 5:13, which says, "These things I have written to you who believe in the name of the Son of God, so that you may know that you have eternal life." That's when it all fell into place for me. Because God had done all that was necessary for me to be reconciled to Him, once I simply accepted Christ as my Savior, it would then be perfectly logical to know that my eternal state was settled. As is customary, the message was followed by an invitation to receive Christ. I silently did that and slipped up my hand when prompted to do so by the speaker. As the meeting broke up, I introduced myself to some of the Bible college students, and inquired about the college, where it was, could I visit, etc. They were very excited and said that they would help me anyway they could. Everyone left in groups of two or three and my female companions and I headed to the parking lot as well. On the ride home, I sat quietly in the back seat alone with my thoughts. There had been no spiritual fireworks, no heavenly visions, nothing remotely miraculous, and yet, deep down, in the deepest part of me, something had happened. I felt different, there had been some sort of change, like a burden or weight was lifted from me. All I could say was, "Wow, thank you, Lord."

EPILOGUE

I ended up taking classes at Florida Bible College, graduating in 1976. I met and married my awesome wife Alice in 1975 while we were both students. After 49 years, two children, and eight grandchildren, we have called Bristol home since 2010. After some years in Florida, Iowa, and New Mexico, we are enjoying the natural beauty of the area, along with all the wonderful friends we've made here. The Virginia Creeper Trail is where we can be found quite often, taking short hikes and long bike rides. We relish each day that God gives us, because each is truly a gift.

ACKNOWLEDGMENTS

This book is a miracle because I'm a miracle. Three years ago, I almost died of Covid. I spent a total of nine weeks in two hospitals. During five of those weeks, I was in a coma. I'm incredibly grateful to the Lord for his goodness in sparing my life. I'm glad he gave me the opportunity to write this book.

Thank you, Victoria, for all the work you did in bringing this work to fruition.

Thank you, Mike, for encouraging and praying for me to keep on writing.

Thank you, Holly, for the time spent retyping the manuscript.

Thank you, Margaret, for the illustrations that add so much to my story.

Thank you, Mom and Dad, for providing a wonderful environment to grow up in, I wish you both were here to read it for yourselves.

Lastly, thank you Alice. I'm sure that you've been praying behind the scenes all along. Love you!